A TALE FROM
ADVENTURES OF RAGGEDY ANN™ AND RAGGEDY ANDY™

The Kite Ride

You can read this book as you listen to the cassette tape which accompanies it.
Turn the pages when you hear the tone signals.

Writer/Producer: Mary H. Manoni   Illustrations: Vernon R. Mc Kissack   Book Design: Libor Pokorny

SVE
SOCIETY FOR VISUAL EDUCATION, INC.

1345 Diversey Parkway, Chgicago, Illinois 60614
A BUSINESS CORPORATION

ISBN 0-89290-059-8   Dewey Decimal Classification: Fiction
Printed in United States of America

D1712298

One day Marcella looked around the playroom and decided that the dolls must be tired of never going anywhere.

Oh, yes, she took them out into the backyard for picnics. But that wasn't the same as really going somewhere.

Where would they like to go, she wondered.

"I'll bet they would really love playing in the park," Marcella thought to herself. "It's such a beautiful day. And they could see all of my friends."

Scarcely had the thought popped into her head, than she scooped up the Raggedies and Scotty and Babette and the tin soldier.

And before you could say "Jack Robinson," she had put them all into her wagon and was soon on her way.

It was a very nice park, and it was only a few blocks from her house. In fact, Marcella passed it everyday on her way to school.

When she got there, she found a happy surprise.

She found some of her friends playing there. And, do you know what they were doing?

They were running up and down flying kites! They were having so much fun.

And they had an extra kite that they said Marcella could fly!

For a little while, Marcella raced with them, up and down the grassy park. Her kite would go up a little way, but it wasn't flying the way she wanted it to.

The dolls lay in the wagon watching. For, of course, they never moved or talked when people were around.

All of a sudden Marcella's kite came down to the ground with a plop.

"Oh, dear," the little girl cried. "Why won't my kite fly like I want it to? Why won't it stay up in the air?"

One of her friends told her he thought he knew what the trouble was. Marcella needed a longer tail on her kite. He said some kind of rag tail would be the very best kind.

"Rags," Marcella cried as a happy thought struck her. "Rags! The Raggedies would be the very thing. But I'd better use only one. More than that would probably be too heavy."

The three Raggedies were so excited they could scarcely breathe.

Although none of them was the least bit selfish, each one did so want to be the one who got to go. They lay in the wagon as still as mice as they waited for Marcella to pick one of them.

Which one would she choose?

But before Marcella could decide which doll it would be, two of her friends suggested that, if it was all right with Marcella, all three Raggedies could go for a ride.

And that's just what happened!

At first they had a few problems making the idea work. It had been easy to tie Raggedy Ann and Cynthia to the tails of the kites. Raggedy Ann had straps on her apron and Cynthia had them on her overalls.

But Jennie wasn't sure how she would be able to tie Raggedy Andy to her kite. He didn't have suspenders or straps. Finally, she looped the end of her kite tail under his arms and across his chest, tying it in the back.

Quickly the wind caught the kites. The Raggedies soared into the air.

As soon as they were in the sky, Raggedy Ann, Raggedy Andy, and Cynthia began to laugh and talk about the great adventure they were having.

They were having such a good time. They didn't notice that the three kite strings had become twisted. Suddenly— plop—Raggedy Ann was blown right into Cynthia's face!

Cynthia was so startled she didn't even try to get out of Raggedy Andy's way.

And, quicker than it takes to tell about it, Raggedy Ann and Cynthia were all tangled up with Raggedy Andy!

All of their weight together was too heavy for the kites.

They began to fall. They couldn't stop themselves. The Raggedies were helpless!

Kites—dolls—came tumbling downward. They crashed into the trees.

How would they ever get out of the branches? How would they ever get back to Marcella?

They were too worried to talk.

But just then each doll looked at the other two. Which one was doing the poking? That wasn't a very nice thing to do.

Each doll was just about to say something to the other two when, peeking carefully out of their shoe button eyes, they saw who it was.

Some robins were building nests in the very tree in which the Raggedies had landed!

And the birds were trying to pull yarn from the dolls' heads to help make their nests!

Now all of this poking and pulling didn't really hurt the Raggedies. They were stuffed with nice clean cotton.

But if the birds kept on pulling, the dolls soon wouldn't have any yarn hair left!

Just then, they heard Marcella calling, "Raggedy Ann, Cynthia, Raggedy Andy— where are you?"

Marcella sounded very worried. And the dolls never wanted her to be unhappy.

But now they only looked at each other. What would they ever do? They couldn't call to Marcella and tell her where they were.

But they wished with all their candy hearts that she would look up in the tree and see them.

And their wishes came true. For she did!

The Raggedies had wondered how Marcella would ever get them down. But it was simple. Because before Marcella could even ask if he would, Bobby was climbing the tree.

Untangling the dolls, he carefully handed each one down to Marcella. And Marcella held them just as carefully.

   As Marcella hugged them,
she promised them over and
over that she would never do
such a thing again.
   But as for the Raggedies,
well they could hardly wait to
get back to the playroom and
tell the other dolls about
their wonderful kite ride.